W9-DDD-239

Published by Semiotext(e)
PO BOX 629, South Pasadena, CA 91031
www.semiotexte.com

Cover Art: Louise Bourgeois, *CELL (CHOISY)*, 1990–93
Marble, metal and glass
120 1/2 x 67 x 95"; 306 x 170.1 x 241.3 cm.
Glenstone Collection
Photo: Peter Bellamy, © The Easton Foundation / Licensed by VAGA

Page 153: © Akademie der Künste, Berlin, Bertolt-Brecht-Archive. Photo: Hainer Hill.

Design: Hedi El Kholti

ISBN: 978-1-58435-196-2
Distributed by The MIT Press, Cambridge, Mass. and London, England

BOOK OF MUTTER

Kate Zambreno

semiotext(e)

for my mother

"As usual when engaged in literary work, I am alienated from myself and transformed into an object, a remembering and formulating machine."

—Peter Handke, *A Sorrow Beyond Dreams*

"He wrote me, 'I will have spent my life trying to understand the function of remembering, which is not the opposite of forgetting, but rather its lining. We do not remember. We rewrite memory much as history has been rewritten. How can one remember thirst.'"

—Chris Marker, *Sans Soleil*

BOOK OF MUTTER

I have this memory. I think I dream about it sometimes. I am 18 years old. I knock on the door of a house, located in the affluent area of my university town. I have responded to an ad hanging up in the student union. An elegantly dressed woman, in her late fifties perhaps, answers the door. Do you know what you're here for? The woman asks while we are standing in the kitchen of the large sunny house. I tell her I do not. I most likely smile, because that is what I did to fill silence with strangers at that age, what I still sometimes do, even now.

She tells me that there is another woman, the one who owns this house. She tells me this other woman has good days and bad days. And I will be hired to help her—somehow. And when she calls this woman by name, she comes to me, her red hands dangling at her side. She is wearing a fanny pack around her waist, as if she were getting ready to travel somewhere.

I am sure I smile overly wide. I look at the woman who welcomed me into the house. I realize I am supposed to speak to her instead. I do not ask what's wrong with this other woman although it will slowly become clear to me, but nothing is ever clear to me, and every day I go there it will be with the wilt and uncertainty of a first day, an interview in which I ask all the questions.

I am supposed to come twice a week. My role is intended to be secretarial, I believe. I return the next week with a physicalized dread.

The woman greets me at the door. The other one, who hired me, is gone. No, maybe she doesn't actually greet me but opens the door and then walks away, leaving it open.

I follow behind her footsteps. She enters each room first. Yet I find myself playing the tour guide. This is the kitchen, I say. Yes, yes, she answers. It is different now that it is just the two of us. I feel I am supposed to reassure her. I pick up a framed photograph on the coffee table. A family smiles back, rehearsed and in matching colors. Is this you? I point at the woman in the center framed by two young boys and a man. She picks up the picture. A tiny smile. Oh, yes, she says. Yes.

I never see anyone else in the house, as far as I know she is now alone. I don't see the husband or sons in the photograph. No one calls for her. I never see the other woman again, the one who hired me. This perceived rupture shakes me. I do not understand it.

I find myself in a bright room that appears to be a converted porch. The sunlight picks up spider webs and dust through the windows. She stands at the doorway. She looks around the room with a worried expression. There are papers scattered everywhere. I realize I am supposed to go through these papers of a former self, a self that used to have her own business apparently.

It is an impossible chore. I am an inept curator. I play around with the piles of paper for hours at a time, rearranging them, moving them from place to place, into files marked with my hand, sometimes placing a scrap or a check or a scrawled missive under her nose, under those eyes and asking her—Do you remember?

At the end of each afternoon she pays me. She writes me a check, ripping it off from her book. Her cow-like cursive so different from the tight neat curlicues I've come to recognize. First I must find the checkbook. The pen. And then tell her what the amount should be. I remember, I am tempted to lie. I am both broke and unmoored. But I remember also feeling the guilt, as if under my skin, my uselessness. My empathy also still there, somewhere, pounding yet tremulous. For she is already paying me too much, for what I am doing, which is nothing.

This experience of failure. How it repeats throughout my life.

You'll come next week? I remember the look in her eyes. She won't remember this moment the next week, the moment when she asks me to return, the end of an afternoon spent together when she now knows who I am. Her life staggering through a series of dark rooms, her large sunny house her labyrinth.

I say I will return, but sometimes I don't, and then I stop coming at all. I don't remember exactly why. I wonder if it has something to do with this sense of not being able to finish the project, of not knowing the project, of not being able to add any order to the chaos, outside of me, inside…

How callous. I just abandoned her. Perhaps this is why she still haunts me.

How can I remember this? It was so long ago. The only thing that can be confirmed are these words on the page, is the way I have told this story to myself and reframed and rewritten it over the intervening years.

All I'm drawing on, a few sense-memories:

large red hands

my stuck uselessness

stairs

In *Cell (Choisy)*, Louise Bourgeois recreated a model of her child-hood home in Choisy-le-Roi, surrounded by a wire cage, with a large guillotine suspended above. The miniature marble house rests on a nineteenth-century workbench, alluding to the family's tapestry restoration workshop in the second-floor wing. The house has since been demolished, replaced by a theater. But Bourgeois has also said, beyond the destruction of the physical structure, that the suspended guillotine represents the need to destroy the past by the present. She has said, "To have really gone through an exorcism, in order to liberate myself from the past, I have to reconstruct it, ponder about it, make a statue out of it and get rid of it through making sculpture. I'm able to forget about it afterward. I have paid my debt to the past and I'm liberated." When asked why the enclosure looks like a prison, she responded, "It is because I'm a prisoner of my memories. I have been a prisoner of my memories and my aim is to get rid of them."

It is an exact replica, she says, you can go inside her parents' room, inside her room...

Over now a decade, my multiple attempts at reconstruction....

I moved home a few months before my mother died, and then we occupied that house in silence. Making our specific sounds, father and daughter, our own closing of doors and walking up stairs, avoiding each other in the house carpeted with cream everything. I had been hit with the uncanny sensation that my mother was haunting the place as I mimicked her movements, folding balding towels.

The house still remains as it was before she got sick. Everything still arranged as my mother had dictated, except slowly decaying or crumbling, losing its place or purpose. Dusty miniature hand soaps shaped like hearts. Corners veiled with spider webs. The ossified squirrel found under the front room sofa years later—the older Croatian woman who cleans for my father once a week hadn't vacuumed underneath for years.

All my childhood I remember my mother cleaning.

Louise Bourgeois's *Femme Maison* series. The illustrated women with houses for heads.

To be a housewife, in the old mold, was to live by the rule of erasure. One's day operating around pretending that nothing occurred, no mark was made. Ordering one's life by rooms. Like Chantal Akerman's Belgian housewife Jeanne Dielman.

Peter Handke writing of the contained and expected life of his mother, "the stations of a woman's life."

We had to remove our shoes. We had to be as quiet as the carpeting.

What my mother feared the most as everything spiraled into chaos, was that she had lost control over her house, which she saw as beginning to fall into disorder, although to outside eyes it was still immaculate.

Oh the house the clean house she moaned. Did she say it just once?

Over a decade later, I still cannot shake it.

I have her room. I sleep in her bed. I piss and shit in her pot. I have taken her place. I must resemble her more and more.

—Beckett's *Molloy*

Roland Barthes sharing an apartment with his mother. In the wake of her death, upon her removal, he finds himself meditating on absence. She infects his writing on photography—she is everywhere. She is everywhere by being unable to be located.

I refused to look at the squirrel. I have a horror of roadkill. The voluptuousness of rent bodies thrown to the side of the road. But in my mind I picture it frozen, as if in surprise.

Lot's Wife immobilized, her mouth wide open.

Don't look back
Don't ever look back

(She wanted one last look at her home, the home she tended to so carefully.)

We lived on Camelot. A chipped white fence announces this in black letters, although for years some letters were missing. The architect of this rather mundane 1960s subdivision in the northwest suburbs of Chicago named it after the Kennedys, my father once told me. I don't know if this is apocryphal, like so many narratives of my family. It always felt like a joke.

Roland Barthes: *History is hysterical.*

I don't know much of my mother's childhood, but I know that her Sweet Sixteen party in Glen Rock, New Jersey, had to be canceled because that was the day JFK was shot. I try to think of my mother as that teenage girl.

From Lady Bird's journal:

Mrs. Kennedy's dress was stained with blood. One leg was almost entirely covered with it and her right glove was caked, it was caked with blood—her husband's blood. Somehow that was one of the most poignant sights, that immaculate woman exquisitively dressed, and caked with blood.

In my memory my mother was this glamorous, remote, somewhat tragic woman. Like Hedy Lamarr.

Somehow that was one of the most poignant sights...

My mother is in my memory this glamorous, remote, somewhat tragic woman, yet sometimes when I close my eyes I see flashes of her on her deathbed, mouth wide open like statues of those saints in ecstasy. Flashes that for years afterwards made me gasp out loud in public.

Don't look back or else you will be consumed.

The electrical taxonomy of memory: Louise Bourgeois's blue antique wooden cabinet stuffed with empty glass vessels backlit with light—perfume bottles, carafes, vases, pharmaceutical jars, silver trays, all once used by the artist. To walk by this installation, to stand before it, when I see it at the Tate and then the Guggenheim years ago, as I travel in pilgrimage before her *Cells*, feels like an act of risk. How precarious they are. How they could come tumbling down.

All the women Louise Bourgeois collected like these fragile glasses, women I also collect, fictional and fictionalized, that I abandon myself to in acts of intense research and investigation—Anne Sexton, Antigone, Marilyn Monroe, Medea, Ophelia, Cassandra, Sylvia, Virginia, Zelda.

Addendum: Barbara Loden, Nella Larsen, Diane Arbus, Shulamith Firestone, Valerie Solanas, Susan Sontag, Kathy Acker, Chantal Akerman, Louise Brooks.

Any woman remote and unknowable. Any woman furious and desperate. I collect them for my mantle.

In my parents' bathroom cabinet a row of Clinique lipsticks in silver cases. All shades of brownish rose, all eroded with her lips' long absence. Today one could open the mirrored cabinet, the invisible line marking His from Hers and those lipsticks would still be there. The remains of my father's favorite saint, her altar of powder and Vaseline, tweezers. The memory of her physical presence, standing there, making herself up. I've got to put my face on she would say. She had to use the lighted make-up mirror that remains inside the cabinet for her fading eyes. No better relics for my mother than cosmetics, my mother who made up her face with such devotion, a ritual that I watched and then was taught to repeat from an early age.

a lock of hair
a piece of bone

my mother my mirror

Anne Carson in her essay, "The Gender of Sound," describes Echo as *the girl with no door to her mouth.*

Sometimes my mouth opens up and my mother's laugh jumps out, a parlor trick.

According to Borges, *apocrypha*, which now means false testament, an account that cannot be authenticated, actually comes from the Greek for *those having been hidden away*.

We called the guest room by her name, although we were too young to remember when she slept there, cast-off daughter from another marriage. It was a room bathed in yellow. Her room. In a framed photograph on the dresser my father's sideburns, my mother with a perm, a smiling blonde girl perched awkwardly. We children never went inside this room. I shared a room with my sister instead. We tiptoed around it. It had the stale air of abandonment to it.

The ancient Greeks imagined memory as a large house. According to the theory, to recall a specific idea or object, one needed to visualize entering the room in which it was contained.

Yet I'm not ready to go through the closed door. I cannot be stumbling around in this house of memories.

My mother is the text. I cannot enter her.

Your mother was not herself in those last few months...
But who was she?

The kitchen was my mother's room, is still my mother's room, all the housewifery—the ceramic farm animals, her baskets. Except the feminine touches have now decayed. The candles lean in their candlesticks, exhausted and broken children.

My breed are dinosaurs my mother would say. Her kind. Like the Anne Sexton poem.

My mother would wake at 5am in order to begin housework. And also, I think, to be alone.

Sylvia Plath would awake at 5am to write before the children awoke.

Sylvia Plath with her head in the oven

Bruloirs—the large ovens that burned witches

the house that has fallen on her

My mother collected hand-woven baskets. They held Christmas ornaments, napkins, her gardening journal, scrapbooks. She even hosted parties where these baskets were sold.

I have not bought enough crap. This is my mother trying to joke, she is in the hospital.

My mother. I know almost nothing of her origins. Was she born in a basket, sent downstream?

Her Nativity scene of ceramic statues.

She owned every one except the pregnant woman with the chicken.

Which she thought was tacky. (Because she was pregnant? Because of the chicken?)

I read in a biography of the visionary artist Henry Darger:

The central fact of his life is that his mother died when he was young.

The central fact of his life.

The central fact of my life is that my mother is dead.

I am Charcot's hysteric: *If you must know, my mother is dead.*

The History of My Life is The History of My Mother's Life. Both a compulsive autobiography, an impossible history. Boxes of scraps, of drafts, of attempts.

When I first began this project, now over a decade ago, I read in this same biography of Henry Darger that he was buried in a pauper's grave at All Saints Cemetery in Des Plaines, Illinois. The same cemetery where my mother is buried. This fact startles me, catalyzes something.

MOTHER is our point of origin. And when she is gone we are home-less. We search for other mother figures to follow, like orphaned Ruth wandering to strange lands just to be mothered.

Go return, each to your mother's house.

There's no place like home.

The Wizard of Oz was Henry Darger's favorite book.

My mother's name was Gale. Like Dorothy Gale.

She called herself an orphan.

Marilyn Monroe was called an orphan to disguise the fact that her mother was in an institution.

"Over the Rainbow" played at her funeral.

I never thought of her as having a life before, of ever being a past wife, even though I know she was married before my father and had a child. A daughter.

Henry Darger's mother died after having given birth to a daughter, later given up for adoption.

His love of books about orphans: *Oliver Twist, Heidi, Little Orphan Annie.*

In Henry's old Lincoln Park neighborhood there is now a park called Oz Park. It is undoubtedly the same park he used to walk through on his strolls down Lincoln and Webster, picking up rubber bands and pieces of twine. Walking through the alleys, hunting for the unwanted. A statue of Dorothy in red shoes greets visitors. I like to imagine this park as a tribute to Henry.

The Wonderful Wizard of Oz was published in the year 1900. Frank Baum had written it while living on Humboldt Park Boulevard in Chicago.

I go to Henry's old haunts. Lincoln Park is now upscale restaurants and boutiques and chains. Yet I can see him, walking around his neighborhood, an old, tired, poor man. He is not homeless but perhaps people sense his stench as that of the unwanted. Perhaps people shy away from him on the sidewalk.

I walk around his alley, taking pictures, I don't know of what. He goes through trash cans. He collects greeting cards, magazines, string, old newspapers and photographs. I pick up a few rubber bands on the street.

During the day he works as a janitor, until he needs to retire. He keeps a catalogue of the thrown away, of the lost and found. He is a custodian of the abandoned in his room at 851 Webster Avenue. I stand outside of his apartment building. I take pictures. I don't know what I'm looking for.

Remington typewriter (1 of 2). Shoes. Broken eyeglasses. About 500 balls of twine. Pepto-Bismol bottles, rinsed out and aligned. Piles of newspapers. Rubber bands in cigar boxes. Clippings of natural disasters and murdered girls. Packets of maple syrup. Stacks of books, including *The Wonderful Wizard of Oz*, *Heidi* and *Oliver Twist*. Magazines, including *Good Housekeeping*, *Life*, *Saturday Evening Post*, *Parents*. Miniature Madonnas. Pictures of Jesus. Mass cards. Pictures of little girls including Little Annie Roonie and the Coppertone Girl. Framed portraits of the Vivian Girls. Art supplies, such as round watercolor containers with handwritten labels. Copies of the Bible. The unmailed letters to the Pope, his imagined correspondence to a higher place. Thirteen volumes of his novel totaling 15,145 pages, *The Story of the Vivian Girls, in What is known as the Realms of the Unreal, of the Glandeco-Angelinnian War Storm, Caused by the Child Slave Rebellion*. 10,000 handwritten pages of his sequel, *Crazy House*. The three large bound albums with fold-outs about 12 feet long and 2 feet wide containing the watercolor illustrations. Thick scrapbooks with pasted-in illustrations. A 5,084 page autobiography, *The History of My Life*. A 10-year daily weather journal.

My father buys anything on sale and available in bulk. Rolls and rolls of toilet paper, paper towels. Containers of blue washer fluid, like embalming liquid, line the garage shelves, a miracle of constancy.

He stays longer now at the cash register, asking the person behind the counter to see if any of the new quarters have come in. He will not notice if she is impatient.

He will stand there at the counter. He will turn over each quarter on his palm. He is looking for a state that he does not have. My father collects these quarters in a special album. A quarter for each state in the nation.

He is a collector, too, like Henry, scavenging in the world for objects to protect him.

My father obsessed with the American Civil War. He knows every important battle, every dot on the map. Our vacations spent visiting Civil War battlefields and burial grounds. Chickamauga and Chattanooga in Tennessee. Antietam in Maryland. Shenandoah in Virginia. Valley Forge and Gettysburg in Pennsylvania.

Childhood summer trips to presidential homes, both grand and humble. Monticello, Mount Vernon, Ash Lawn-Highland. The creaky wooden floors of childhood shacks of former presidents, standing behind a fraying velvet rope to behold a tiny bed covered tight in an ancient white blanket. So and so slept here. Up and up creaky wooden staircases.

My father now travels by himself. He shields himself with his sensible windbreaker while puttering around Civil War battlefields, state capitol buildings.

Henry Darger shared with his father an obsession with the American Civil War. His fantasy epic *In the Realms of the Unreal* collages Civil War and world war imagery for his rainbow-violent battle epics staged by the Vivian Girls against enemy soldiers.

My childhood vacations spent stopping at bronzed signs, pausing for a moment, getting back in the car.

Toes lined up, staring at relics and ruins.

While I am still living in Chicago, teaching at the community college. Every time I visit my father I drive past my mother's grave. I do not visit her there. But all I have to do is pull the car into my mother's spot in the garage to witness these relics of my mother, the abandoned watering can, the place between the car and the wall where she used to crouch a nicotine fugitive, the rubber yellow gardening gloves my father now wears. My father began gardening that spring, with every aching bend reenacting his wife's years of labor. But he is not as meticulous as she was, and many of the plants have died and remain brown and buried within their pots.

If writing is a way of collecting, even hoarding memories—what does it mean then, to also wish to disown?

They have reconstructed Henry Darger's room at the Intuit Gallery in Chicago. Where he sat in his third-floor apartment at 851 Webster Avenue and lived inside his fantasy world for decades, writing thousands and thousands of pages. Collaging, painting, drawing, fantasizing. Speaking his character's lines in different voices.

He does not allow himself to be censored. Though his 5,000 page autobiography is mostly about a tornado named Sweetie Pie.

His shrine on his mantle. A doll-like Christ child peering out at me from a calendar for May's Grocery & Delicatessen. An image of the statue at St. Vincent's Cathedral in Lincoln Park, where Henry attended Mass up to five times a day.

Cut-outs of the models for the Vivian Girls, a framed photo of a Christ child, a crucifix, three icons of the Virgin Mary. All those eyes. These are the sacred images he would both worship and direct his rage towards.

The first time I returned to her gravesite, a couple years after her funeral, it happened to be around Memorial Day. I walked around the cemetery and took pictures of the objects left behind, the bouquets of flowers, the teddy bears, like a treacly gift shop for the dead.

I read somewhere that the beautification of death movement began in the mid-eighteenth century. Cherubs and cheerful poems were now placed on headstones as opposed to what adorned them the century before

(morbid poetry)

Day-glo bouquets in the shapes of crosses. Garish planters in the shapes of lambs and swans dot the landscape. The detritus of the dead.

Souvenir. French for to remember.

To put these memories in a book, so as to be released from it. These thirteen years of it. Like a sacrificial offering. To bury it in the ground. Writing as a way not to remember but to forget. Or if not to forget, to attempt to leave behind.

All the offerings left for the dead
so they remain buried.

—

The notes Roland Barthes began to write the day after his mother's death. His mourning diary. His elegiac, spare meditations on grief cut up into fragments (how she, the mother, is in fragments). The quartered typewriter pages he kept on his desk, scraps he would write on with pencil and ink, all while writing this other work on photography. How the mother also suffuses this other text, as he thinks through how a photograph is a sign of absence, what is not there.

What does it mean to write what is not there. To write absence.

The moment Barthes meditates on what it is he's compiling.

Oct. 27
Who knows? Maybe something valuable in these notes?

Walking around Louise Bourgeois's *Cells* at the Tate Modern, these massive chambers enclosed by wire cages or scavenged wooden doors from demolished or abandoned houses. The doors opened slightly, peering into the spaces you cannot enter, the experience like inhabiting the strangeness of someone else's dream, these memory rooms that preoccupied the artist for two decades. A tableaux of sculptural objects, like glass spheres, arched bronzed figures, fabric screaming heads, her phallic bronze fillettes, clasped hands, along with antique mannequins, clothing and furniture, and silence. I stand outside looking through the white French doors circling the space. Inside she has hung on skeletal metal frames and hangers her once-worn clothes in somber monochromes: mournful blacks, and threadbare and translucent whites, almost swaying with the drafts of the space, as if the bodies they housed had evaporated.

My mother's mirrored closet upstairs, the door on rollers, that familiar rattle and boom, the bedroom door was always closed, we were never allowed in there. An archive still carefully preserved, rows of my mother's past, the faintest of scents still clinging, a mixture of detergent, hand lotion, cigarettes, towards the back the plastic shrouded dresses, towards the front the delicate sweaters, slacks, never new.

In the years afterwards, I begin to sneak home souvenirs. A black skirt with three fading gold buttons on the side. It doesn't fit me. My white flesh spills over the elastic waistband. My mother was a stretched-out version of me, tall and thin. A skirt I have never seen her wear, perhaps from her secretary days before she met my father, when she was a young single mother, those hard days occasionally alluded to, days of tomato sauce on crackers. I can taste the salt of my mother's past before I ever existed.

When we were younger, she almost never allowed herself new clothes. She cooked and cleaned for us, did everything for us...

Only when I grew older, came into consciousness, did I realize my mother had some mystery she carried around with her. Some past left inarticulate. Did she nurse her secrets tenderly? Did she give them a name?

I cannot interrupt her in her silent statuary. My still-wife.

Yet my mother is the love-object, the object of my curiosity and desire.

Violette Leduc channeling her mother at her memoir's opening, trying to imagine the girl-maid impregnated by the boss's son. The obsessive desire to tell, to report, to circle around.

No mother can ever have been more abstract than you are.

How fragile she began to look in the last few years, growing more beautiful each year, her girlish figure even slimmer, who knew that it was the cancer, turned on, slowly eating away. In the last years of her life my mother took on the appearance of a consumptive, almost radiant.

But no, I go through my box of photographs. The two of us on my graduation from college. A few years later—me with my mother when I'm taking a master's degree. She is wearing the same cream dress with flowers. The same cream dress with flowers that—. The same cream dress with flowers (I can't, not yet). In the second photograph, months before we knew (did she know?), she looks drawn, haggard, quite thin. She looks ill. Not beautiful as I remember. Could both memories be housed inside of me?

My mother, exhausted and rent, curled up in the dressing room at the Ann Taylor at the strip mall. She wanted to *splurge* and buy me an outfit, to acknowledge my new staff writer position, even amidst everything she was going through, she still wanted me to be a girl who dressed at Ann Taylor, not a girl who wore thrift shop clothes, so I acquiesced, to please her. I would have done anything for her then. She bought me a pair of beige trousers that were too tight and pinching at the waist. Afterwards we ate at the Panera Bread next door. I ate…a sandwich? She sat there in the booth, hunched over her coffee, which she didn't drink. Is that where she collapsed sobbing? Or in the changing room at the clothing store? Unthinkable, that my mother would break down in public. I remembered this was the last day we attempted any excursions. The last day we tried to act normal.

I wore those beige trousers while conducting a day-long interview sometime in those months, when my period came. Hunched over on the chair, my reporter pad at my lap, bloated and cramped, unfastening the top of the trousers so I could breathe. I had to tie a sweater around my waist to go home. The crumpled pants remained on my bedroom floor, hardened with blood at the crotch, until I finally threw them out.

I am going to erase this.
This doesn't belong here.

I began buying clothes when my mother died. Clothes that made no sense. Disposable, frivolous, trendy things. A purple T-shirt dress. A bright green wool skirt. A black shirt with a pink heart sewn into it.

The triptych of Gertrude Stein's *Tender Buttons*: Objects, Food, Rooms. William Gass described these divisions as *things external to us, which we perceive, manipulate, and confront, things which nourish us,* and *things which enclose us.*

Yet the objects we collect, they can nourish us too.

In *Camera Lucida*, Barthes circles around what he calls the Winter Garden Photograph, the picture of his mother, Henriette Barthes, when she was five years old, with her brother in the winter garden. He sees the essence of her innocence and her kindness in this image.

I cannot reproduce the Winter Garden Photograph. It exists only for me. For you, it would be nothing but an indifferent picture, one of the thousand manifestations of the "ordinary"/ it cannot in any way constitute the visible object of a science; it cannot establish an objectivity, in the positive sense of the term; at most it would interest your stadium: period, clothes, photogeny; but in it, for you, no wound.

One baby picture of my mother hanging in the upstairs hallway. Tinted blonde hair, tinted yellow dress, tinted blue eyes. A happy baby. Generic.

I cannot find her there.

And then those years ago I received in my inbox an email from my sister, sent to my immediate family, containing a link to my mother's sixth-grade class photo. The Alexander Hamilton School in Glen Rock, New Jersey. Is this tall black-and-white blur of coke-bottle glasses in the back row really my mother?

My sister must have been searching for any sign of my mother online. All this we will never speak about.

My mother who disliked having her picture taken. You can tell also in this blurry class photo, this eerie archive from the past. Her teeth are bared, but she is not smiling.

Barthes writes about searching to recognize photographs of his mother from when he was not born. A labor he calls Sisyphean. *I never recognized her except in fragments.*

My mother used to tell me that she would iron her hair to straighten it as a teenager, and I would picture her folded over an ironing board in the basement with the iron she used to press my father's shirts. My mother always in my mind surrounded by these weapons of domesticity.

The sizzle of hair burning from the curling iron. The hot anger of the hairdryer.

Let me go I'm drying my hair she would say to me on the phone years later. When we would talk each day. She would call to check in on me. She would ask me whether I left the house, whether I was eating, whether I was sleeping. Try to smell the roses today, Katie, she would say.

I always wanted to stay on longer. I have always wanted too much.

In those years afterwards, when I am at the house without my father (he is out of town, I am feeding the fish) I sleuth around for information. In the bureau that used to hold our board games I find two photo albums I have never seen. Polaroids from before my parents' marriage.

Barthes flipping through photographs of his mother, trying to locate her, knowing the futility of such a task.

He wishes, he says, to write a little something about her, so that she will be remembered.

The subject lovely in bell-bottomed blue jeans and a red top. She is holding two oranges in front of the grove and laughing. I remember that laugh. How tremendous and throaty.

She is standing behind a skinny man wearing a white floppy hat, her arms embraced around him. They are on a beach.

She is wearing an orange bikini and, with a young girl, she is burying the man in the sand.

Palm trees. They must be in Florida visiting her parents, before she was estranged from them, before the divorce.

She is posed in a white tennis dress and a tennis racket, hair in pigtails, on a lawn in front of a home, blinking against the sun.

My mother with a shiny sixties bob, like Lady Bird Johnson. Her husband has black eyeglasses and a tie. Posed with their blonde darling on the sunny sidewalk. They are the All-American family.

Someone else's mother. Someone else's wife.

With regard to many of these photographs, it was History which separated me from them. Is History not simply that time when we were not born? I could read my nonexistence in the clothes my mother had worn before I can remember her. There is a kind of stupefaction in seeing a familiar being dressed differently.

I find in one of the boxes a Ziploc bag containing a sepia-toned photo of my mother. Her high-school portrait. Perfect bob. Peter Pan collar. Her expression tranquil. There is a rip across the nose.

I study this photograph. Her tweezed eyebrows are uneven. Yet so manicured and put together. I recognize that about my mother.

I put my ear to the glossy image but no sound comes out.

I look at these photos, try to guess their secret histories.

The man taking her photograph caught her laugh, when she crinkled up her face. She looks happy here, but of course photographs can lie.

My mother in front of a car, the sky reflected in its windows. Her pensive lovely face. She is wearing that same white floppy hat.

It's true that a photograph is a witness, but a witness of something that is no more.

Henry Darger made scrapbooks out of coloring books and telephone directories. He pasted in source materials, pictures of young girls that would become the models for his Vivian Girls, the leaders of the child-slave rebellion. He especially liked Shirley Temple. Little girls like blonde, blue-eyed dolls. Stand-ins for the unknown sister given up for adoption.

A smiling girl in blonde pigtails perched awkwardly with my father in sideburns, my mother with a perm. (I too had Cindy Brady pigtails, I remember their tight hurt.)

She came to live with us for a short time when I was eight or nine. She was a teenager then, maybe eighteen, and she appeared at our doorstep all teased hair and leather jacket.

I would plot in my dear diary how I would overthrow this usurper. I don't know why she left. I remember screaming fights in the middle of the night.

So she left and I never saw her again.

That's a lie.

Even now I don't like writing about her. I put down my cup of coffee, I pace around, I think, why not excise a character from this family drama?

He searched for her everywhere. He hung up pictures of her on his walls. He drew her picture over and over. He collected her from comic books, coloring books, magazines.

My pain is the hidden side of my philosophy, its mute sister.

The Aronburg Mystery that runs throughout *In the Realms of the Unreal.* The mystery of a theft of a newspaper photograph of Annie Aronburg, his heroine and leader of the child-slave rebellion.

She is based on a photograph from the *Chicago Daily News* of a murdered five-year-old girl named Elsie Paroubek. Her photo and a notebook of his writings were allegedly stolen when Darger lived with a group of fellow hospital workers.

His alter-ego, Captain Henry Darger, looks for it in libraries. He threatens God that if the picture is not returned by a certain time he would go over to the dark side, which he finally does, taking up with the Glandelinians. But before that Henry went to mass, offered up novenas, said rosaries. He even erected an altar to Annie Aronburg in a friend's barn.

At one point his identification with Annie became so intense that he took on her name.

My father became obsessed with archiving my mother after her death. Like gardening, he picked up her hobby of scrapbooking. He enlisted my sister to put together a book of his travels with my mother, after his retirement. Alaska cruise ships. New Mexico. Asheville, North Carolina.

There was one photograph my father remembered taking with my mother and his cousin Rosie, in front of this building shaped like a giant basket that was the headquarters of the basket company in Ohio. Going to the headquarters was her pilgrimage, my mother joked. My father became fixated on finding this photograph. He became so determined that this photograph should be in the album that he made the trip up again, in his widowed solitude, and asked a waitress at a nearby diner to snap a photograph of him standing in front of the building.

At Rosie's wake (liver disease), there were those now ubiquitous scrapbooks to flip through, along with the poster boards of photographs. A diversion from the dead body in the open casket.

My father found his missing photograph in one of these scrapbooks, and while the wake was still going on, he removed it, and took it to a nearby drugstore to be reproduced. My father finds nothing eccentric about his behavior.

Rosie once worked as a beautician at a funeral parlor, her own thin hair dyed black and curled and puffed, the white scalp peeking through. Her last job was as a cashier at a Meijers, before she was too sick to work. She lived with a woman who we called Cousin Diane, Diane tall and taciturn in blue jeans, Rosie extremely short and stout and brash, like that branch of the family, but also generous and sweet, like the Italian cookies she made, despite being severely diabetic, also like the women on my father's side, who so often have their limbs removed. Rosie and Diane met while working at the Motorola factory, putting together telephones. Diane had lung cancer the same time as my mother. Diane and my mother were always smoking buddies, standing up in my grandmother's kitchen, ashing into that old pewter tray. She lived longer than my mother, but shrank down to almost nothing. I remember the shock of the open casket at Diane's funeral. Why an open casket? I still don't understand. To confront death? There was no way her shriveled corpse could be made to look beautiful. Although it never looks beautiful. Always like a completely different person. An alien with permed hair and bad makeup.

We put together one of those poster boards of pictures of my mother at her wake too. Memorializing as a crafts project.

(my mother's was closed)

My father did not want to include any photographs of my mother smoking. Or in her bathing suit. Although in the summer my mother was always in a bathing suit, that pink one-piece, showing off her slim figure, tanning. Mowing the lawn, a cigarette dangling from her lips.

The family portrait hangs above the television in the living room.

I am 13, 14. I wear a royal blue dress. I am arranged awkwardly, move this way, that's right, now your hand on your knee, look this way, that's right.

My mother sitting, knees this way, I am seated next to her, my sister and brother are standing awkwardly at the sides, with my father at the center. His arms rest on their shoulders. The solemn patriarch.

Smile please.
We are frozen. My mother is gritting her teeth.

Rosie once told us about a family who wanted a family portrait with the recently deceased made to look like he was still alive, and she propped open his eyes with toothpicks. I remember her telling the story, her eyes twinkling.

His illustrations of the Vivian Girls hung framed on his wall. A fictional family.

Nearing the decade anniversary of my mother's death, I am living in North Carolina and looking at *cartes des visites* of the dead in the special collections room at Duke University. I've exhumed this book on my mother again, after a few years away from it, after being frustrated with how out of control it became, its illegibility, its seemingly inherent failure. The work now containing the ghosts of its own archives, its past iterations and echoes (alongside other ghosts, the ghosts of American history). I don't know whether it's because of the anniversary, or whether this timing, as it usually does, plays some more unconscious role. It doesn't seem possible sometimes I will ever finish it, or what that even means.

I have begun a new period of research, this time with photography and the Civil War. I am interested in these two parallel histories— the relationship of this relatively new documentary form with this national trauma, where there was so much death and horror, the war and especially slavery, this trauma still unhealed. Postmortem photography a part of the mourning and memorialization process, often the only time loved ones ever had their photographs taken. These images were hung in homes, sent as copies to friends and relatives, worn in lockets or carried in pocket mirrors.

This was not considered unduly morbid.

He holds her up with one arm. She looks like she's falling over. Like she's had too much to drink.

Caption: Till Death Do Us Part

Having exchanged vows before photography was discovered, this image serves as the only visual document of their marriage.

It is the mid-70s. My mother and father are young, beaming. My father holds my mother. My mother holds a scotch and a cigarette.

In the collection, a box of albums of stickers from one Mary Horton, one of the largest collectors of such card albums. The cut-out illustrations known as scrap pictures, or scraps, used to embellish. The albums are arranged by seasonal and thematic pages. Everything cheerful. Sentimental. I realize the day I look through them that it's Valentine's Day.

cupids
hearts
lace
flowers
a page of fans
a page of smiling Victorian ladies
Christmas

Assemblages were considered a lady's accomplishment in the 19th century.

My mother's carefully produced scrapbooks of our childhoods. The stickers she used so similar to Mary Horton's scraps. (Archive your memories! Bleats the sign at the strip mall.)

After my mother died my father didn't want to let anything leave the house.

If you want anything, take it—my mother whispering to me. Take it now. Maybe she suspected the embargo that would occur afterwards. He eventually let us make copies of our childhood photographs.

Scrap:
My mother holding our baby brother. Me and my sister on each side, holding our own baby dollies in our arms. Our white Easter shawls. Playing firm little mommies.

for you, no wound

The three of us all young and tan, like sleek field mice. Upturned faces at our mother, usually hiding behind the camera, only sometimes spotted as a sleeve of rabbit fur or the mirror reflection of a tall glowing woman. All my childhood I remember my mother hating to have her picture taken. So in many of these photographs she is not present at all. But I know she is there, my maternal ghost, omnipresent, so I love even the ones in which she does not appear.

An unknown person has written me: 'I hear you are preparing an album of family photographs' ... No, neither album nor family.

At the library I look at photographs of dead babies whose eyes are open as if they are awake, or made to look like they are sleeping. That one looks like she is peacefully snoring.

We take great pains to have miniatures of Deceased persons agreeable and satisfactory, and they are often so natural as to seem, even to Artists, in a quiet sleep.

A mother and baby side by side
They look so tranquil

my stillborn manuscript, which I didn't know how or where to bury

The old swing at the cabin is new. My mother stands me up on it. She kisses my cheek. I am a baby in white. I stare with my blue eyes blankly, too young to register the goings-on. My mother is gorgeous. Slim legs crossed. Softer skin. She is wearing denim shorts and a pale turquoise top with white flowers. Against the window you can see the ball of light of the flash. This time my father's the ghost. She kisses me. She kisses my soft, plump cheek.

I loved having babies, my mother confided. Lying there in the center of the living room. I don't know why she felt compelled to confess this. Why then. At the end of everything. I loved being pregnant.

I had a desire to get pregnant when my mother was dying. To get fat and flush and round. I wanted to give her a grandchild. I wanted to give her a baby to hold. Then all would be all right.

I would name her Mommy. So when she was gone she would still be with me. My baby alone. My dolly.

Violette Leduc channeling her mother in the opening of her memoir, desiring to swallow her up whole, to cannibalize her.

Let's go back again, open your belly and take me back.

The way grieving a parent can alter our memories. The memories of our childhood now rose-tinted.

How to prevent the sentiment that comes with intense grief, the writing over?

Henry was obsessed with protecting children. Perhaps he wanted to protect his child self that had to fend for himself in the asylum, or his unknown sister given away. He founded along with his only friend William Schloeder a "Children's Protective Society," that would put up abused children for adoption, a vision never realized.

And yet his armies of naked girls with penises are beautiful and surreal and more than a little unsettling. There is a biographer that theorizes that he was a serial killer, a child molester, that he had kidnapped and murdered Elsie Paroubek. Or at the least read his artwork as somehow exorcising violent fantasies. Others hypothesize that perhaps Henry didn't understand anatomical differences between boys and girls, maintaining his innocence.

There is something here I want to say, about private art practices being held suspect, but I don't know exactly what.

I save the photos I took of the *cartes des visites* on my desktop: deadbabies.pdf.

Kill your darlings
a phrase used often in connection to editing one's own writing

Or: kill your babies

How and why to take out the cherished, the sentimental, these protestations of innocence, that which you hold onto too fiercely?

All likenesses taken after death will of course only resemble the inanimate body, nor will there appear in the portrait anything like life itself, except indeed the sleeping infant, on whose face the playful smile of innocence sometimes steals even after death. This may be and is oft-times transferred to silver plates.

We are at the cabin. I am just out of the lake. Rainbow towel wrapped around my neck. I am lean and awkward in my adolescence. I am wearing a two-piece, black with hot pink stripes. Pink bug bites stilled by a cross from thin nails. I do not yet have braces on my teeth. Our hair is cut the same, my mother and me. Feathery bangs, frizzy in heat. I hated that haircut. I hated being your tiny twin.

My mother and I are laughing, caught in an embrace. She is smiling at the camera. At my father. I am nuzzling against her red T-shirt, overjoyed at this gesture of affection. My mother must have just gotten up from her desk in front of us to take the picture. The desk faces the window, which faces the lake. She was reading, watching us splashing in the water. And I have come in.

On the desk the mise-en-scène of my mother: paperback mystery novel, crossword puzzle, coffee cup, full yellow ashtray, nail polish remover, plastic bag with manicure supplies.

Her arms around me. Tan. Strong. Lawn-mowing arms. (When they melted away into bones and bruises she mourned their loss more than any other part.)

Black and gold memorial cards were popular during the Civil War, usually bearing some poem, shilled by various companies.

Dearest mother, thou has left us,
Here is thy loss we deeply feel,

And I, my mind in turmoil, how I longed to embrace my mother's spirit, dead as she was! Three times I rushed toward her, desperate to hold her, three times she fluttered through my fingers, sifting away like a shadow, dissolving like a dream, and each time the grief cut to the heart, sharper, yes, and I cried out to her, words ringing in the darkness: 'Mother—why not wait for me? How I long to hold you, so even here, in the House of Death, we can fling our loving arms around each other, take some joy in the tears that numb the heart.'

Embracing shadows. Virginia Woolf uses this gesture of inarticulation from *The Odyssey* in *To the Lighthouse*. In Woolf's novel, Mrs. Ramsey is there, and then she is gone. We do not get a death scene, we have arms wide open to nothing in the middle of the night.

TIME PASSES—this is what Woolf writes after Mrs. Ramsey dies. Woolf writing of her mother trying to write of her mother not being able to write of her mother.

The merged skeleton of the 19th century conjoined twins at the Mütter Museum in Philadelphia that I saw years ago. I stood before it for some time. How intimately they leaned into each other.

The stuffed pink figures of Louise Bourgeois, curled around each other. Are they cadavers or anatomical dummies or. They are a family or. Her two black headless dummies wrapped around each other. They are on display in a heavy piece of wooden furniture. One of them has a wooden leg.

I climb into the hospital bed, I curl into her, like I am hugging my skinny child, like we are one, once again. I cry into her backbone, How am I going to live without you?

my mother my sworn enemy my first love

And then I promise her tearfully, I will write book after book and I will dedicate them all to you.

She is whom I write towards. She is whom I must expel from my body. Must resurrect.

It was on his journey home in 1908 after escaping from the Lincoln Asylum for Feeble-Minded Children that Henry saw the weather event that would shape his personal mythology. He claimed he walked back from the farm to Chicago on foot, more than 100 miles. During his journey he witnessed the tornado that hit Tampico, Illinois. Barns and windmills smashed and demolished.

In the memoir he wrote at the end of his life, after the first 200 pages of early years, his autobiography becomes almost 5,000 pages of a fantasy epic featuring a monster twister named Sweetie Pie.

I began to attempt to write to make sense of all of these different memories and tenses of my mother. Was, is, was... It infected everything. I kept on trying to write her down. My dead mother wormed her way into every book I have ever written. I kept on trying to erase her from the pages, change her into other mothers.

And how this thing has expanded and contracted over the years—my mother book, my monster book.

In his watercolors always a storm cloud threatening to erupt and destroy an idyll. Rain down fear and terror onto his innocents.

Later in his life Henry kept his *Book of Weather Reports*, documenting fluctuations in the temperature up to three times daily.

Friday October 30 1959
Cloudy and threatening during most of the day. Rain sets in near 4 o clock in the afternoon. Off and on rain all night. 5 a.m. 44 11a.m. to 3p.m. 50 degrees

My mother's name was Gale. She disliked it.

Her sensitive, shifting patterns

The violence of Erika Kohut in Elfriede Jelinek's *The Piano Teacher*. She tears at her mother's hair, the dyed pieces coming out in a clump in her palms. Her mother who kept her under surveillance. Her mother who dictated what she should wear, where she should go.

I have had that mother. I have hated, I have loved that mother. Like the girl's mother in Duras's *The Lover*, tearing at her clothes.

In the morning my mother laid out our clothes. Matching garishly patterned outfits from the mannequins at Kohl's or Carson's. These clothes humiliated me.

Every day after school we would place our schoolbags on the kitchen counter, and my mother would go through them.

She insisted I go to the school dances. Every day she quizzes me—have you been asked yet? (Why is my brother excluded from these popularity contests?) I wear my sister's hand-me-down dresses that fall off my now-voluptuous breasts. I get pictures taken with boys with Biblical names.

It always seemed impossible, to resist her.

Louise Bourgeois's *Maman* spiders—devouring, claustrophobic, all-encompassing. Her mother the chief seamstress in the tapestry restoration business.

Where'd you get that? Even once I was an adult my mother would zero in on an unfamiliar garment, nose wrinkling, no nuance of her daughter escaping her.

Are you lying?

My mother had a nose for anything unsanctioned. Scraps of paper pushed into my white schoolgirl's desk—any grade that was not immaculate. But how could I think of hiding from her, it all came out eventually.

Are you lying?

She stood us in the corner
to think about a confession

It is the waiting I remember most, my stomach nervous and cramped

What happens there is silence, the slow travail of my whole life. I'm still there, watching those possessed children, as far away from the mystery now as I was then. I've never written, though I thought I wrote, never loved, though I thought I loved, never done anything but wait outside the closed door.

She would become possessed. We were her possessions.

Once afterwards she took me to the mall and bought me a new pair of earrings at Claire's. They are plastic and turquoise and triangles. She held my hand and dabbed her eyes with her nicotine-stained tissues. I forgive her anything.

If I talk to you, I may break everything. But, that's not my fault; I can be very, very sorry afterwards.

The women in our family threatening to maim or kill each other, often as a joke or expression of affection. I have inherited their brutal language. My mother: *I'm going to take you out back and shoot you Katie.* My grandmother: *Come over here so I can slap you.*

Luce Irigaray: *If we continue to speak the same language to each other, we are going to reproduce the same history.*

Suddenly, a shock that penetrates even the roots of your hair: in the big room on the table lies the manuscript, with, on the first page, only one word, 'Mother,' in large letters. She'll read it, guess your purpose, and feel hurt.

A sense of betrayal. My sacrilege of thought.

My mother a glorious Clytemnestra in chinos and feathered hair.

the beast, my mother, my love

Have you really not forgotten what it was like there? how everything there fluctuates, alters, escapes…you grope your way along, forever searching, straining…towards what? what is it?

We are again at the cabin. My mother and I are alone in a boat on the sparkling blue lake. It is a moment of calm between us, of intimacy. You are either hot or cold, my mother tells me. You are either up or down, never in between. I don't know why she is telling me this.

—My childhood was unhappy.

—You had a wonderful childhood.

—That is not what I remember.

—But look here, at this photograph. You are smiling. You are happy.

We never remember the moments our pictures are taken.

We think we do, but we don't.

Photographs do not reflect the turbulence underneath.

I am wearing the earrings in that school portrait, there, I still have the haircut like yours, in later school portraits you dressed me like you, in that matching sweater with the turtleneck, and the gold brooch with my initials, you never understood why I was teased.

My teeth are bared in the picture, like I am smiling. But am I smiling? I look like I am either grimacing, or baring fangs.

I would write little suicide notes and stick them in my schoolgirl desk. This is how I would communicate to her, my mother with her fortress of fierce moods and remove. How old was I? I could not have been more than ten years old.

We never talked about these notes, although I know she read them.

I think I'm beginning to see my life. I think I can say, I have a vague desire to die.

The intense beauty of the red room *Cells*. There is the parents' room, surrounded by mahogany doors, with the red bed in the center. The child's room, with sculptures of clasped red hands, spools of red thread.

Louise Bourgeois has said her casts of clasped hands that she makes repeatedly are her spiritual self-portraits—conjuring up something of the intensity and desperation, not only of childhood, but of being an artist.

Hiding in my closet feeling the clothes surround me, protect me. The pleasure still, of folding into myself. When I have gone on attack. When I feel under siege.

Writing is how I attempt to repair myself, stitching back former selves, sentences. When I am brave enough I am never brave enough I unravel the tapestry of my life, my childhood.

Louise Bourgeois's mantra for making art:
I DO
I UNDO
I REDO

The UNDO is the unraveling. The torment that things are not right and the anxiety of not knowing what to do. There can be total destruction in the attempt to find an answer, and there can be terrific violence that descends into depression...In terms of a relationship to others, it's a total rejection and destruction. It is the return of the repressed. I take things away. I smash things, relations are broken. I am the bad mother. It is the disappearance of the love object. The guilt leads to a deep despair and passivity. One retreats into one's lair to strategize, recover, and regroup.

I am a monster child housed in a prim container. (Why, it only exacerbates everything. The nuns, then my mother at home.)

Henry was beaten by the nuns.

Our pathographies: As a child Henry would set fires. He got into fights. He threw ashes into a girl's eyes.

I hit too because the violence chokes me.

Violence the last resort, when one has no language.

My childhood utterances—I cannot shape or discipline my speech, no one understands me.

Henry Darger made strange noises that irritated others.

Words thick with my saliva. I read promiscuously but do not speak real words. I must go to a speech therapist, who eventually sets them free from my mouth.

Even now I can't make language do what I want it to. Over the decade I've attempted to sculpt this book. It's not malleable enough.

I still can't communicate.
I am struggling to communicate.

The perfect lines I must make with my penmanship. I cannot stay inside.

I am not a robin I am a bluebird in the slowest group.

I get bad marks for a dirty desk. I store everything in my desk because I cannot bring the mess home with me and so the nuns dump my desk in the center of the room and I must clean it up to stares.

clean up this mess
clean it up

It is a return, always, to the forces that shaped me. These forces I have swallowed like knives.

On her deathbed my mother crying: *Why wouldn't the little girls play with Katie? Why didn't anyone want to play with Katie?*

As a child I retreat into fantasy worlds.

I am Mother Nature. I wheel around my coterie of ants in our red wagon. I speak to them in my mother's garden. (Is that possible? Wouldn't I have gotten too dirty?) My mother jokes for years that I used to kiss the worms but I deny this vehemently. I am probably just up close, so I can listen to them.

I am alone in the yard. I command the wind to blow through the trees. I talk my secret language.

Neighbors heard Henry speaking to himself in his room, acting out his world in different voices.

He was called Crazy as a child.

As a child, Henry's original diagnosis was self-abuse, which biographers suspect to be a euphemism for masturbation.

Another doctor diagnosed that *Little Henry's heart is not in the right place.*

I sit in English class and pretend that I am the secret heir to the throne, and I nod with superiority at my unknowing subjects.

My freshman year I eat my bag lunch in the bathroom stalls or not at all. The oil-soaked paper bags piled up in my locker, the rotten apples and smashed PB&Js. I still have nightmares about that stench in my locker, the sickness and panic of being found out. (Why didn't I just throw it away?)

Later on Henry began to keep a daily journal, a documentation of his mental weather, the onset of his tantrums fierce and unwavering like the tornado he named Sweetie Pie.

Mad enough to wish I was a bad tornado.

He would threaten to throw the ball of twine at the Sacred Image on his mantle.

Louise Bourgeois throwing sculptures across the room in fits of temper.

I am the bad mother.

Was art for both of them—a form of exorcism, to be able to channel and control, their abandonment, their past? A form of survival.

My mother telling me, lovingly, You are just a square peg in a round hole Katie, a square peg in a round hole.

When I am a little girl she rushes in to defend me, my strangeness. Little Katie cannot color inside the lines. God, my mother says staunchly, did not color inside the lines.

I am happiest with my Barbie Dolls. I play with them throughout high school. My sister and I playing God, exercising agency over our universe of Barbie Dolls with their tip-toe feet and chewed-off hands. We behead them at will. We give birth to teenagers of impossible proportions. Operating fast fingers so fast we act out soap operas, sex games. Their mouths meet each other furiously. We are authors of elaborate tales.

Why wouldn't the little girls play with Katie?

I wonder sometimes if I would have found my own way if allowed.

Like Freud's Viennese hysterics, perhaps I rebelled by breaking down.

The guilty way she would drive me to school-mandated therapy, she would sit outside in the waiting room, or outside on the steps, smoking. My therapist wanted my mother to come inside the office, but she refused.

Was she afraid that they would say she was a bad mother?

My mother my enemy my best friend

And yet the second time I broke down, my mother was the only one to catch me.

divining, through her own past, some deep, some buried, some quite speechless feeling that one had for one's mother at Rose's age. Like all feelings felt for oneself, Mrs. Ramsey thought, it made one sad. It felt so inadequate, what one could give in return; and what Rose felt was quite out of proportion to anything she actually was. And Rose would grow up; and Rose would suffer, she supposed, with these deep feelings…

I can still feel her cool hand steadying me in the shopping mall.

The doctor says he wants to admit me to a hospital and administer Electric Shock Treatments. The medicines are not working properly, I am not working properly. I am flattered by this attention. I am in awe of my demonic possibility, like I am Sylvia Plath.

Diagnostic he says. Do you see how fast she's talking? How sped-up she is?

The doctor speaks to my parents instead of to me. I have so many pills inside of me and I am spinning, spinning, spinning. *You will always be spinning your wheels* he later threatens.

My father glumly clutches a brochure. Later he will say to me, incredulously: this sounds like anyone.

My mother has her leather handbag on her lap she is twisting tissues dotted nicotine yellow.

We're taking her home with us, my mother says—and that was that. My father agrees to pay for therapy again for a short period. The pills I eventually flush down the toilet.

The blur of language. I still cannot catch it.

Then we all get in the car and my mother says, *Well what about Grandma Mary?* And my father snorts and waves that away.

And it turns out that my great-grandmother who died before I was born was institutionalized for some time (this is on my father's side).

Natalie Wood's mother on the rocking chair in *Splendor in the Grass*: *A psychiatrist! I can't believe it's that serious. She's bound to get over it in a little more time. There hasn't been any mental trouble in either of our families.*

Years ago, as I first began attempting this book, I a
at the Lincoln Museum in Springfield, Illinois call
Lincoln: First Lady of Controversy." The opening gl
the bed from her stay in the sanatorium. It is a m   ᴐden
frame with antique white bedding. Mostly the exhibit contains
her dresses, her china and silver from the White House, some
photographs and letters.

The electronic sign at the entrance:
How did it come to this?

*She was a Southern belle; wealthy and well-schooled. Suitors vied for
her hand. Abraham Lincoln won it. She moved in the most powerful
circles in America. She was fashionable, intellectual, and spiritual.*

*But in 1875 her only surviving son had her declared insane and
institutionalized.*

How did it come to this?

At which point the letters break up and fly away.

As if evading the question.

Around the same time I went to the Mary Todd Lincoln exhibit, beginning to become obsessed with her insanity trial, I begin to question my father about my great-grandmother (*gathering evidence*, as Thomas Bernhard writes of his process of memoir). She was institutionalized in the 1930s following her husband's death.

Her sons signed her in to the state institution at Manteno, where she stayed for six years.

but she pretty much agreed to it (as much as she could agree to anything)

When Mary Todd Lincoln's eleven-year-old son, Willie, died in the White House, she went through a tormented period of mourning. Her husband warned her that if she didn't snap out of it he would have her committed.

At the Lincoln Museum, the children's play center is called Mary Todd Lincoln's Attic.

She would have tantrums. My father tells me over the phone. He doesn't want to talk about it, although to my father's credit when I push he tries to be forthcoming. *She used to rip things, and she used to smash things, because she couldn't handle the situation, you know?*

I ask him what kinds of things. *Photographs,* he tells me.

She called my grandfather (her son) up one day and said I'm better, and he said Okay.

Mary Todd Lincoln who was holding her husband's hand as he was shot to death.

It was the son who signed her away, signed her away for her growing eccentricities, which he considered an annoyance and a blot on the family name.

It was not a secret. We didn't hide it. None of this stuff was a secret.

I find out my grandmother Mary's daughter too, an Aunt Anna, was institutionalized for most of her life. The black-and-white photograph hanging up in the upstairs hallway of my parents' house. My paternal great-grandparents standing sternly. Little boys, my grandfather and great-uncle, hold a large American flag over their laps. The baby is your Aunt Anna, my father tells me.

It wasn't a secret. None of this was secret. My father insists.

Beginning in the 1940s Anna moved around from private to public institutions and spent the last years of her life in the infamous state institution at Elgin. *It really isn't something the family is happy talking about.* My aunt writes me in an email. (My grandmother is still alive.) She still however is, like my father, reticent yet forthcoming, still fulfilling their role of the family historians.

My father tells me, warily, that as far as he knew she was *difficult.* She couldn't concentrate, he was told. She couldn't learn. She was always running away. One always had to watch her.

You will always be spinning your wheels.

The rebellious daughter hidden in the cellar. The fast daughter or slow one. Her history exiled into silence.

I am like Louise Bourgeois, a runaway girl.

You are the id of your family, a therapist later told me.
ID—to identify.

When my mother got sick and everything spiralled into shit—when she was locked up in the mental ward, under restraints, wasting away from chemo, still enraged, my sister told me about a woman she read about who after her cancer diagnosis torched her house.

I have been your slave! She screamed at us, in front of the mirrored closets in the hallway, as she crumpled into herself.

What at the end made her scream in such rage?

a bronzed figure on the bed—the arch of hysteria

The scream does violence to the throat, which is suddenly turned into a hole, as if there were no other way out but to break through a wall.

Cassandra muttering incoherent screams. Her seizures.

Sometimes when I think of those months—when I let myself I rarely let myself—I feel the guilt rise up like black bile, like the Furies chasing me.

Cassandra sputtering uncomfortable truths. For Cassandra was the real daughter of Clytaemnestra, both women assassinated for their violence and chaos.

I would like to set the house on fire.
The crowded theater of my mind.

Each of us has their own rhythm of suffering.

The document of her decline. The panic attacks. A memory on repeat, as if I had performed it, once before. (They gave me a photocopied handout on panic attacks, they sent me home, I stumbled through the rain.) We'd find her, sitting on the floor in the garage.

She would hide cigarette butts all over the garage in plastic grocery bags. She'd sneak them, then anoint herself with cheap vanilla lotion, to hide the smoke fumes. The sweetness covering over everything

to psych herself up to leave
the house

(I cannot enter it. Yet when I'm inside, I cannot leave it.)

I have known the body of my mother, sick and then dying...

Curled on the couch in her gray sweat suit. She couldn't stop crying now, a whimper and wail, her body soft and weak.

She offered herself up to the altars of Western medicine.

My father tearfully exhorting my mother to get up from the wheelchair, a wailing, weakened Lazarus. She needs to walk, if she cannot walk the oncologists won't see her.

The director Carl Theodor Dreyer put his actress Renée Falconetti through hell. A theater of cruelty.

He made her repeat scenes over and over again.

I have been your slave!
Was this her protest? her private mutiny?

I have been your slave! I can see her crumpling to the floor.

In the film Artaud is the gentle handsome monk Massieu (but how he withered after the sanitorium, hollowed and mad).

The film reels thought lost, recovered in the closet of a Danish asylum.

When she found out she cut off all of her hair.

I will not wear a wig! My mother defiant. I REFUSE to wear a wig. She wore a black knit cap instead, going to and from chemotherapy like an increasingly sickened robber.

Did she refuse the false act? Did she wish to go out into the air open and wounded?

(Dreyer forbid all makeup on set.)

Before, she went frequently to the hairdresser. She got her nails done regularly. Her favorite nail color was Smoking in Savannah, a frosty salmon.

Towards the end we took her in a wheelchair to her hairdressers, to have her face waxed. Hirsuteness a side effect. No longer could she gossip and laugh. No one spoke to her. They treated her like a pariah. These women who later sobbed at her wake.

Renée Falconetti as Joan of Arc
her real tears as her head was shaved

In the silence of an operating room, in the pale light of the morning of the execution, Dreyer had Falconetti's head shaved.

Is this why I cut my hair so close to my head? So that when I look into the mirror I see my dying mother?

I pay tribute to her, my Joan of Arc. I cut my hair short, little patches of white scalp shining through.

Do I cut my hair for penance? My act of self-flagellation.

A twinning between myself and my mother. I perform her on my body.

She was beautiful and severe. The illness brought her a sort of elegance before it destroyed her.

My mother who looked like Hélène Cixous towards the end, all hooded eyes and sharp cheekbones.

(As the tears ran down her face, Dreyer gathered them up with his fingers and put them to his mouth.)

I wipe my face with paper and her image appears.

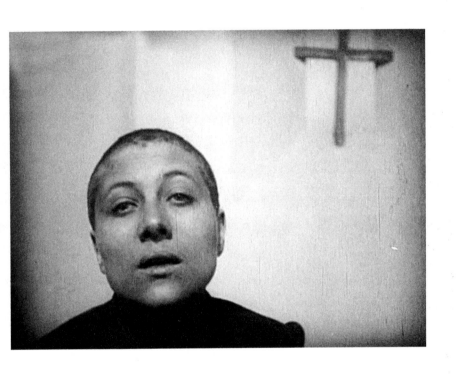

My father sees himself as the authority of my mother's illness. My father has kept it all written down, a record he still consults. He goes through the facts, scratching his head, trying to locate what he missed, what went wrong.

Like the quarters he collects, one for every state. He inserts each fact into his memorial album.

My father swears by his facts recorded in his notebook. In those early years we compare vivid, constant memories. Although I often, in recalling what happened to her, confuse order. I have forgotten names. Dr. This. Dr. That. A rolodex of doctors, a different face each time stuck onto the same useless body.

Henry Darger's weather journal he kept faithfully for ten years, recording fluctuations in temperature up to three times a day.

In them, Henry questions the veracity of official reports. He sits in judgment of the weatherman's authority. The entries grow terse, unbelieving at his pagan prognostications, the forecast a clouded prophecy. He said, He promised—a forsaking father. *Prediction of weather true. Report of thundershower not true. Prediction of weather slightly misled.*

It is not the facts that I search for. It is something ineffable about my mother that I search for. What I want is amber and green glass and gold. Like her eyes. Our eyes.

Yet when he offers up new intelligence, I seize upon it.

My father tells me that when she found out she cut off all of her hair. Although now we think she knew before yes she must have known.

That is not likely my father says with a grimace. My father cannot imagine my mother carrying secrets. Yet I know, she carried them as close as grudges. Secrets my mother carried in her purse with her leather cigarette case which she would open with a clasp of sureness.

We trace through actions yes she must have known before well maybe my father concedes but when? We retrace the months of inconclusive doctor visits, her agonizing pain. We can do this for hours. It is our exhaustive pursuit. For it is only the two of us who can speak like this, my father has become my intimate, or he always was, we get stuck in the basement of my childhood home, going over everything.

She was most worried about how she would be remembered, he now tells me.

The blare of the ambulance siren.

The late-night trips to the emergency room, my mother vulnerable and scared in her paper gown in the naked stalls.

She pulled out the pump surgically installed into her arm.

My father's accounting: six trips to the E.R., one on Christmas Eve.

The lobby of the hospital, that site of perpetual return. Arranged like a living room. The shabby gold lamps. The blood-colored carpeting with psychotic patterns. The grandfather clock. The waxy plants with fingernail moons on the leaves. The earth-colored geometrics in wooden frames. All while stoic nurses in pale blue scrubs hurry to the booming god of the beckoning intercom, through the maze of swinging doors and body-less wheelchairs and dazed patients waiting on beds, peeking out through horizontal bars, refugees of the hospital hallways.

We find her sprawled disoriented on the brown tiles of the kitchen floor.

She claimed she took all of her pills at once, which she had been storing up.

The doors of the emergency room slide open, open.

Q. Why did you leap from the tower at Beaurevoir?
Q. Did your voices advise you to jump?
Q. Did you intend to kill yourself?

My father's accounting: Two months in the psychiatric ward, under suicide watch and lock and key and passcodes and family only.

She has been detained. Forced to wear paper dresses.

My mother, now on antipsychotics, which morph her into a groggy monster. My mother, her thickly slurred apocalypse.

My mother's arms held in restraints, stretched-out limbs bearing purple maps of hell.

My mother, mumbling catatonic for days, while we sit outside her room on hard-backed chairs.

Your wife/your mother has been acting out. She has been misbehaving.
She has grabbed a nurse's necklace.
She has bitten my sister's hand.

The attendant, usually a nursing student, mostly kept to herself, frightened of my mother. A succession of stern or bored or shy female faces that read their anatomy textbooks, reducing the human being to dissected body parts. They would read their textbooks, and watch their patient's choked and grasping sleep.

Waiting, waiting. For something to happen. Something to break.

Palliative care. My father spits out as if the phrase itself was poison. No, your mother is going to live.

Radical treatment.

I hate you and after this is over I never want to see you again I scream at my father. I am screaming to save my mother from all of us. Save her from her treatment. For a percentage rolled into another percentage.

I want to blame my father. That my father just wanted someone to do the domestic work, the dirty work. All hell broke loose when she ceased to be Functional. To be: Wife.

Now I realize that my fury at my father's complicity, his trust at the time in the doctors, stands in for the guilt that I feel for my own. What I allowed to happen to her. My capacity for conformity, seeded deep within my childhood.

On the doctors' advice, we agree to have my mother declared incompetent, so that she can be given shock treatment, so that she can be shaken out of her psychosis and go back to chemotherapy, which she does not want.

We are given a video to watch. It is an amateurish video from the 1970s on electroshock therapy. Something about synapses.

Yet my mother was ultimately saved from shock treatments, only because she was too close to death.

I open my mouth to scream. No sound comes out. Like Helene
Weigel's mute maternal wail in *Mother Courage*.

She is stripped of her clothes.

They have broken her. We have broken her. We have broken this strong, proud, mysterious woman. Broken her of her will. Broken her of her secrets.

Dreyer made his actress kneel on stone floors for hours.

Submitting to the shouts and the spits. She never made another film again.

All my life I remember her on her knees cleaning.

My sister and I take her to the shower. We wash her gently.

Naked legs shaking under paper.

That famous photograph, grainy and fluttering. The naked women like fairies in the forest, almost dancerly. On their way to the gas chamber. These once-brides stripped bare.

An image seared in my mind. My mother and these masses. Like a double exposure.

This conflation itself a sort of crime. (I do not know where to place my mother in the vast catalogue of history.)

When Barthes nursed her he saw her as his daughter.

You become my child, Mother...

For a decade my aunt nursed her invalid mother, my grandmother, paralyzed in a wheelchair.

The warm wet smell of my grandmother's skin, her wrinkled yellowed fingers.

One can be paralyzed by one's own mother too—Emily Dickinson who didn't leave the house when her mother Emily Norcross became an invalid.

I tried to nurse my mother. If I had known then what I know now—that she would die in mere months—I would have nursed her more. I would have abandoned myself to her. I would have given up my life, thrown myself on top of her, tried to crawl inside of her. I was there, but sometimes I wasn't.

Sometimes the fear would creep in and I couldn't get out of bed, couldn't force myself to see her defeated in her hospital bed. Or I threw myself into constant work at the paper.

But when I was there I demanded complete sovereignty over her body. My sister would fly in from California on the weekend and we would fight for a bruised arm, pulling on an emaciated leg.

Oh, but when I had her to myself. I didn't know I possessed such reservoirs of love. I lavished her with my love, all the love that I had been storing up since my childhood, when my mother was a prickly, mysterious, sometimes affectionate, extremely formidable woman who preferred her time alone.

I tried to mother her. I tried to mother her as she was not mothered.

Now she had no choice. It had broken her. We had broken her. I massaged her chapped body with lotion, I helped turn her, helped change her.

I imagine myself Shirley MacLaine to my mother's Debra Winger (didn't everyone say she looked like Debra Winger? the dark feathery hair the sharp features the reputation of being *difficult*).

I demand a sign be posted on her door: Be careful. This patient is fragile. She bruises easily.

We were never intimate Mother and Children while she was our Mother—but Mines in the same Ground meet by tunneling and when she became our Child, the Affection came—

I brought one of her purses to the hospital. It sat on the table next to her bed. It was black with a gold clasp. She guarded it fiercely. It was the only thing she could hold onto, something that was hers, something that reflected who she used to be.

In the purse:

a used tissue
a sample hand lotion
a lipstick never used
a wallet without money
crumbling brown tobacco lining the bottom

no mirrors

One of the charges against her was idolatry.

They tricked her into physicalizing her apparitions, her watchful saints.

They demanded exacting details in an attempt to force her to betray her visions.

Q. Do your saints always wear the same dress?
A. She is wearing a cream sweater with a turtleneck and a shiny gold brooch with her initials. Her jewelry was always so cold, so hard and so cold.
Q. Do they have hair?
A. Yes she has hair. Had hair. It depends. It depends.
Q. Is their hair worn long?
A. I can close my eyes and reach out and touch it, her helmet, sprayed so carefully. I pat it and it has all the brittle softness of a sparrow.
Q. Do they have arms and legs?
A. When her muscles melted oh those arms, those tanned, beautiful arms, she mourned them more than any other part.
Q. What languages do they speak?
A. The language of bronchial smokiness and the language of New Jersey whininess and the language of knowing bemusement and the language of mild sarcasm when addressing stupid counter clerks and the language of scream and come here.

She signed an abjuration:

I, Joan, called the Maid, a miserable sinner

A confession of guilt
Yet the cross next to her signature was a sign the document was to
be ignored. She appeared in public in women's clothes.

She was forced to wear a shift and a hat that had been inscribed:
Heretic
Apostate
Relapsed
Idolater

She went back to her cell, put on men's clothes

Death was preferable to betraying her self

*I never intended to deny my apparitions, and whatever I said or did, it
was because I was afraid of the fire.*

Charred at the market square at Rouen. They lifted up her robe to
make sure she was a woman.

Underneath the glorious stained glass ceiling of St. Vincent's, Henry's church in Lincoln Park, besides the enormous stone altar, there is the statue of Mary cradling her adult son in her arms, as he is taken off the cross.

The framed photograph in Henry Darger's reconstructed room of a mother holding a baby boy. A stand-in for his mother, an image he found somewhere.

I cradled my mother in my arms in the hospital bed, my mother once so proud and independent, now so frail, body yellow with bruises. I bathed her lovingly with my tears.

She is thy mother; thou shalt not uncover her nakedness.

I was now the mommy. There was not much of her left.

I can't stop people from saying what they need to say. I don't know how to stop repetitions like these.

Every year, I revisit it.

I don't want a living wake! My mother moaning, barely cognizant. Yet the dutiful daughter opens the door, she ushers in the peanut-crunching crowd shoving in to say goodbye. The parade of previous years, of past grudges. This was your life.

Every year I am that numb girl again.

What I remember is that spring was beginning to be born and my mother was dying.

I tried to make her comfortable. I got her little things to eat. Her body was so strange now. Curiously heavy. She was covered in sweat. I changed her so it would be light and cool over her now leathery skin. Changed her like a doll. Like a child.

I turned the bed to the window so that the sun would come in, so she could see green outside, life outside. Her face lifted.

My hyacinth girl.

Like a labor. (Why is it always a labor. We struggle to be born. We struggle to die.)

When she was dead I thought it was a dream. That I did not witness what I did. That I would wake up.

Her mouth wide open like the statues of those saints in ecstasy.

Helene Weigel's silent scream comes after Mother Courage hears the shots offstage that kill her son Swiss Cheese. The head thrown back, the mouth open grotesque. Based on a photograph Brecht had seen of a woman in lament over the death of her son during the Japanese shelling of Singapore.

All of the action comes to an abrupt halt.

The ivory dress with the flowers and the elegant scoop neck she bought especially for my college graduation. I grabbed that dress from her closet upstairs, along with a pair of worn-out beige panties and sheer pantyhose, the kind she bought at Walgreens in an egg. My mother would never have worn that dress with bare legs. That was my first, absurd instinct as soon as it was over—the jolting train ride of the death rattle, the elaborate labor, the pushing and pushing, dabbing my mother's sweaty brow, feeding her morphine in a little dropper, more and more and more, until a sudden final tremendous groan—to find something for my mother to wear. How can you plan an outfit that will last forever? Until, of course, it rots away, along with the body it sheathes, which I try not to think about, although sometimes it makes me start up with panic as I am getting ready to sleep.

The men come and take my mother away. My mother's t⟨
towards the television screen. On her deathbed, the h⟨
erected in the living room.

The men close her eyes and place a sheet over her. Me burrowing
into my uncle's shoulder, imploring them to be gentle with her.

She is delicate. She is so skinny, look how thin she is, thin and
bruised arms like a young winter tree.

The pamphlet dropped off by the people who came and took my mother away...

What to expect:
Sometimes mourners can expect physical symptoms. Headaches, stomach pain, loss of appetite, intestinal upsets.

When I began working on this book, two years after her death, I began experiencing bodily disturbances. Numerous painful and humiliating tests and specialist visits without a conclusive diagnosis. Indeterminate pelvic pain. One particularly violent attack I'm screaming and sweating for hours, in the bathtub, giving birth to nothing. I wonder if the neighbors think I am being tortured. It was only later I recall that it was the anniversary.

Maybe the body remembers what the mind wants to forget.

The woman who comes with her clipboard and her latex yellow gloves she snaps on one at a time.

The woman who flushes all my mother's medicines down the toilet. Who removes all of my mother's waste—the paraphernalia of the dying.

Some psychological symptoms of grief:
Shock
Despair
Sadness
Humiliation
Yearning

I wonder if I will ever stop yearning.

An anniversary that takes place over two days. The real day and the official day. The first date is the date she actually died, the day we watched vigil over her long labor into the eternal night. The second, the date my father recognizes, the official date proclaimed by the official woman who got to the house officially after midnight to tell us, yes, she's officially dead.

So I will call the day after, I know this is when he will memorialize her, in a more formal, public way than the daily way we have privately mourned her these years, our mourning tucked into our shirts and into the way we stand. This is the date we vocalize to each other.

I know he will have a Mass said for her on that date, even though she stopped going to church in the last years of her life.

Although she became devout at the end, didn't she? her frail head lifted to receive the circle offered her.

Jane Bowles who converted to Catholicism on her deathbed, while being taken care of by the nuns in Málaga.

I am Jewish you know. The deathbed—the clichéd time of confessions at the end of one's life.

Did she ever confess to anyone? Did she ever confess her life?

I was alone on that last night.

She was there as well.

No she wasn't.

Yes she was. The one you've tried to excise from the family album.

I too have inherited this disease of estrangement.

I never know when to be subtle or explicit, what to take out, what to suggest.

She is not there for the illness, for the five months of agony. My sister has called her in the last week, I do not know how she reached her. For me she disappeared. Now she returns at a time when my mind cannot process her, to the death-theater of my mother.

My father sits in a chair. He doesn't think the time has come. She is the one holding my mother's other hand. The hairsprayed perfume of her permed blonde hair. She is the one to witness this with me. An uneasy sisterhood.

Allegedly Darger researchers must agree not to dig up the family secrets. Not to locate any surviving relatives who might claim the estate.

No attempt has been made to trace the sister who had been 'given up for adoption.'

And what happens afterwards? What happens to the ones she left behind?

TIME

PASSES

She hit me. My sister, the one I grew up with, has taken us to a bar in West Hollywood and the two of us, the eldest and the youngest, are drunk on gin and tonics that we have had her pay for. We are sunburnt and drunk and mildly belligerent like the trashy girls that we are, that we grew up with, that Mount Prospect girl with her harsh edges I can never completely erase, that she embodies before me. And we sit on the steps the two of us and smoke just like on that night when it was the two of us together and there is a trial, a trial of my mother for her sins her first-born sees as unredeemable.

I shrug uncomfortably. The past is past.

He hit me. Just that once.
I watch the memories play across my mother's face.

I say that to her now. My mother said your father hit her.

She shakes her head vehemently. Never. In her history book my mother is not the victim, my mother is the villain. My father probably, too, but we do not talk about him.

Why was Mom like that? Months earlier we are at my mother's wake. She is in front of my mother's closed coffin. She is talking to my mother's best friend.

Not a day went by that she didn't think of you… this woman is saying. Why was Mom like that?

We think that your mother was…this woman is saying. They are blaspheming the dead.

At the wake I fetch my sister, the one who comes in between me and the one who is not me. I say something like, You better get her to fucking shut up.

For I am also the violent one.

My mother once told me she was so hard on me when I was a teenager because I reminded her of herself.

I need films to fill in her backstory.

When I think of my mother's teenage years I think of Natalie Wood in *Rebel Without a Cause*. Some story about a boyfriend with a motorcycle. Of working a job as a roller-skating waitress. Or Barbara Loden as Ginny Stamper in *Splendor in the Grass*.

And then when I think of my mother in her young married life, living in western Texas, with her military high school sweetheart, I think of Barbara Loden in her 1970 film *Wanda*, playing the eponymous Scranton housewife who abandons her family, who has been set adrift, who even finds herself in a botched bank robbery.

I can see my mother squinting against the dust storms in Odessa, stern and closed, like *Wanda* making her way a white ghost through the mountains of coal. And then alone with a baby afterwards, finding her way to the dull Midwest, working as my father's secretary.

I always thought of my mother as a vagabond. Drifting until my father came along and saved her from her hard life. The joke is that he courted her with groceries, this struggling single mother, sticks of salami and heads of lettuce.

Not a day went by...

I know that there was a trial. And this other daughter chose to go live with her father, most likely because my parents had already remarried and quickly started a new family. We rarely spoke her name.

That trial scene in *Wanda*. Appearing at court, late, with her hair in rollers, having just bummed money for the bus ride, mumbling to the judge that her children would be better off with their father.

When I was in college, my half-sister took a job waiting tables at the pancake house about a mile away from our house. (She can't be Wanda stuck in a string of useless jobs. She can't be Ginny Stamper taking up with gas-station attendants to get a rise out of her mother.)

As I learn later, once they discovered that she was working there, my mother and my father went to see her. And she told my mother that unless she could apologize for what she did to her, that she should not return. I don't know whether she was referring to what we talked about, or something else, a deeper level of hurt and abandonment.

I picture my mother in this scene. My mother, her stomach twisting with anxiety, like when she waited on the stoop outside my therapist's office. I picture my mother with her nervous tissues, pushed inside her leather Coach purse, one of the only luxuries she allowed herself. I can still see her walking with one of her purses on her arm, the other arm swinging, her long legs overreaching and I must hop and skip to catch her.

And then my stomach twists and even though I know I am wrong I hate, I hate, those who weighed her down with guilt and grief. I see my mother with tears in her eyes. My mother who feared any confrontation. My mother with her grudges. With her disease of disinheritance.

A series of undated photographs in the album I discovered. My father, mother, and uncle are at a party. The clothing tells me it is the 70s. My mother and my father pressed against each other laughing in a conga line. My mother sitting playfully on my father's lap.

If the chronology is correct she went from Wife to Wife, from Family to Family.

Did my mother wonder like Mrs. Ramsey: *But what have I done with my life?*

Mrs. Ramsey who represses her own memories: *she had had experiences that need not happen to every one (she did not name them to herself).*

Perhaps this is grief—the inability to recover someone. For when someone is alive, there's always the hope of accessing, of having someone reveal themselves to you, over time.

I'm not very deep Katie my mother would say, gaily. Almost as if to keep me from guessing.

I place the photo of my mother in the white floppy hat next to an image of Wanda hesitating before the courthouse.

In my mother's bedside bureau, that I have now ransacked many times, there is a collection of papers. Our school papers, report cards, crayon drawings, the assorted memorabilia of our lives. My fourth-grade school report on Hitler's last days in the bunker (Eva Braun was blonde, she bleached her hair, they took cyanide which smells like almonds). My paper on Ulysses S. Grant, with a stenciled patriotic cover in plastic. At the back I have drawn a hideous crayon rendering.

My mother was the custodian of our childhoods.
Of her life all I have are apocrypha and memories.

The photographs of my mother's parents, who I never knew, hang in the upstairs hallway. They are like me, like my mother, pale with dark hair. My grandfather, who died before I was born, has a sharp bird nose and a mustache. He wears an army uniform. My grandmother's tweezed eyebrows and cupid bow mouth. She was estranged from my mother all of my life. I don't know why. I know that she died the year before my mother's illness, and my mother found out because her brother called to ask for money for her burial (my mother carried this with her, she didn't tell anyone, she swore my father to secrecy).

All my life I thought my mother was born and raised in New Jersey until she ran away and eloped at the age of eighteen to marry a man not my father.

Now my father tells me she was born in Brooklyn, and then moved to the Bronx. My grandmother worked in City Hall and gave out licenses. My grandfather, Louis from Austria, was a truck driver. There is one more framed photograph, my grandfather as a boy, in his knee socks and brooding stare playing the violin. He looks like a young Franz Kafka.

My father now tells me as we stand in front of these photographs that my grandparents were buried in Star of David coffins. He finds this deeply bizarre.

Your grandfather was a Catholic, my father scoffs. This doesn't make any sense to me. My father is silent. Your mother was furious, he finally says. My father has always said this to me, my mother's mother was a liar, she lied about everything...

Kafka: *Today it occurred to me I did not always love my mother as she deserved and as I could, only because the German language prevented it. The Jewish mother is no "Mutter," to call her "Mutter" makes her a little comical...*

Henry Darger has filled out his family tree in one of his Bibles. An invented family mythology. A wife named Margery. Under children he writes that one little girl disappeared a month after his wife died.

Henry Darger's origins are mysterious as well. He told his neighbors that he was from Brazil and that his surname was Dargarius. He might also be from Germany.

My father tells me over the phone at a later date (with an audible sigh, I keep on interrogating him) that when he met my mother he assumed she was Catholic.

She went to Mass with me and she seemed to know what to do. Would you like to be baptized? My father says the priest asked when he met with my parents before they married.

Sure, said my mother. (That rings so much like my mother, the casual, monosyllabic answer.)

I now pronounce you.

What disturbs me is how little my father knew about my mother before they were to be married. My father interested in my mother for her present tense.

My mother like a young beautiful Robin Vote in Djuna Barnes's *Nightwood*, converting religions, changing with whatever partner. A passivity I cannot reconcile with the independent, solitary woman I knew.

My father claims not to remember any details of the baptism.
Did your family know about it?
Yes. A long pause. We were sworn to secrecy. She said please don't tell anyone, I don't want my mother to know.

One learns to hide oneself from one's mother.

Antonin Artaud: *We are born, we live, we die in an environment of lies.*

The night my mother died I sat outside on the front stoop smoking, attempting to compose my mother's eulogy. In my shock I felt sure there was something about my mother that needed to be heard. I did not save the pad of paper. It is not in the archives.

Peter Handke writing in elegy to his mother, *cheated out of your own biography and feelings.*

She swore she had no ambitions. Only when she was younger, she told me, she wanted to be a June Taylor dancer.

She majored in political science and would not tell my Republican father who she voted for. I know she voted for Ross Perot.

She never received a college diploma, which was a source of shame for her.

She loved the Beach Boys. She loved to dance.

She was on a women's bowling team. She had many friends—both of my parents had many friends.

She was good at crossword puzzles, because she had studied Latin.

She liked to go off by herself. *I'm going gallivanting.* Window shopping but not buying. She would sit at a diner counter and order coffee and pie.

She had a tremendous sweet tooth but didn't eat much else.

She hated meatloaf, it was her mother's recipe. She made it when she was in a foul mood. And so it always tasted—fraught. Fraught yet tangy.

She learned to cook from a roommate who was Italian.

She had never been to Europe.

She was learning Italian on a tape recorder in the kitchen for a trip to Italy my sister and I were going to take with her, which would have been the summer after she died. My father never took her to Europe. He had seen it in the Navy. Why would I want to go there again? he would say.

When I was younger she would take me to visit several of my father's elderly aunts who lived alone. I don't know why I was always the one on such errands to nursing homes. She would bring them little gifts, sit with them, have coffee with them.

Have I forgotten to record my mother's essential kindness?

My father insisted on giving the eulogy. But he had nothing prepared. Instead he stood up at the altar and crumpled into tears.

It belongs to him, as much as his wedding.

Cluckings at the funeral luncheon. Take care of your father. Take care of your father. Everyone turned to me with glistening eyes, stabbing at pound cake on paper plates.

Without a wife my father was lost. He was Mr. Ramsey in *To The Lighthouse*, leaning on any available woman. He had never lived alone before. He went from his mother's house to the Navy to married life.

I remember pulling a yellow legal pad out of my father's desk in the weeks afterwards. Here. I said. Write everything down that you have to do today. When I would stop by to visit him, I would see the notes scrawled on his pad.

Take walk
Water plants
Groceries

Although his health is increasingly frail, almost every day now my father still takes a walk, either around a nearby lake he drives to, circling around twice, or around an inside track if the weather dictates. Or sometimes, lately, just around the neighborhood. I took my walk today, he'll tell me when we talk on the phone. Let me see, what else?

I see my father puttering around a track. Every day is a track he traces around a certain number of times until the day is done.

Henry Darger tracing his Vivian Girls out of magazines and coloring books. Tracing his visions pinning them down into a two-dimensional world. Despite his hallucinatory fantasy world of a war-ridden Oz, Henry lived an ordinary life to outside eyes. Or extraordinary only in its thrift, its routine, its solitude.

I think about the need to document, to pay witness, to record. The hoarding of facts, like some sort of proof.

Towards the last years of his life Henry keeps his daily journal, mostly abandoning his diatribe against the weather gods. Most of the entries are repetitions, an old man going through his paces. Same thing as yesterday. He attends up to five masses a day, he takes up to three walks, he collects balls of twine, has tantrums.

He catalogues his world, in an attempt perhaps to control, to contain his fierce mental storms. He has many attacks of temper, followed by penance. *A Sorry Saint I am.* The journals function as his apologia. *Had a tantrum to day. Did a lot of swearing—I'm sorry.*

Sometimes in his journal Henry is penitent, although often he is obstinate. *I'm a hardboiled egg and will always be one.* Sometimes he says a Novena to court favor.

At the end of the notebooks his handwriting grows shaky. In the winter of 1968 his tantrums become again directed at the weather. His left leg aches all the time. His hip also. He has been bumped by a car. He has trouble getting around.

And every note in his journal, his work on his life history, his visionary landscapes, that nocturnal world, everything a totem against his mortality, his pain, his being tied down to his small existence. His art, his work, his writings a way to escape from the cage of his failing body.

After my mother's death I find, in a basket on the top of the refrigerator, two bound notebooks decorated with illustrated roses. My mother's gardening journals. The only example of her handwriting except recipe cards and calendar reminders. And what a jolt it is to see her handwriting, this intimate trace. Like Henry's weather reports they rarely veer into her interior life. In it she records travels, temperatures, nature sightings (rabbits and robins), the progress of her plants and flowers, and occasional long-term chores around the house. It takes a chatty, although impersonal tone, occasionally veering into exclamation points. She writes an entry about every week or every other week in the spring for several years.

Then there is her last entry, dated two months into her illness. The handwriting faltering. It's difficult to say how she made it up the stairs to the kitchen to pen this note.

Diagnosed with lung cancer. Lost all life as I knew it. Got E's plants and are trying to keep alive. Early snow. Can live with it. If alive in spring—
TRELLIS in FRONT DOOR POT
Blue Hydrangea!

Lost all life as I knew it. She is one of her dying plants she is trying to keep alive. A final entry, strange and haunting. I don't know who E is. I am continually confused by the exclamation point after Blue Hydrangea!

After this my father's hand appears. He continues the gardening journal, in some way altering the significance of the archive.

He must stay in bed. He is now always under the weather. He stops his daily journal. Nothing to report.

Henry mourns his life. An entry entitled From February 1971 to December 1971:

I had a very poor nothing-like Christmas. Never had a good Christmas all my life, nor a good New Year, and am now resenting it. I am very bitter but fortunately, not revengeful though I feel I should be. Now I am walking the streets and am going to mass as usual. What will it be for me for New Years 1972, God only knows. This year was a very bad one, hope not to repeat it.

Hope not to repeat it. We know he won't. His journal ends along with his life.

He had to leave his room, his space of fantasy, and move into a bed at St. Augustine's, run by the Little Sisters of the Poor. The same sickhouse where his father died.

That's when the landlord and others went through his apartment at 851 Webster Avenue, his museum of the orphaned. That's when the watercolor paintings for *The Realms of the Unreal* were discovered.

His artworks were not found posthumously, as is often believed.

They slashed open the bound works to sell the paintings individually, disturbing the order of his master narrative, the interplay of text and image. They now rest in pieces in museums.

At the beginning of tracing these connections, I go several times over the course of two years in search of Henry Darger's grave.

I call the cemetery where my mother is also buried. There is no Henry Darger here, a female voice tells me. A pause.

But there is a Henry Dargarius…?

I take down the information:
All Saints Cemetery East
Section 6 Block 13 Grave 19

It is muddy, having just rained. I stomp around and cannot find his gravesite.

One time, it is the end of winter, and I borrow a shovel from my father in the attempt to clear what I later realize is not the correct headstone. I tell him I'm doing research on an outsider artist buried at All Saints.

Good luck, the ground is still frozen my father tells me. He hands me a shovel, my mother's pair of yellow gardening gloves black with use and dirt.

The symbols are too potent, as is the symmetry.

The next time I make an attempt, it is about a year later. I go to the main office at the cemetery, the old structure demolished, over the years rebuilt sleek and modern. I print out a map from a kiosk. I speak to the clerk at the office. There is no card for a Henry Dargarius, but he sketches out a map for me.

I still can't find it. I go home, research Darger fan sites online, and finally find directions. The Old People of the Little Sisters of the Poor plot is Block 20, not Block 13. The cemetery office's documentation is incorrect.

I am told to look first for a statue of Saint Hilary (the patron saint of exiles). Turn your back on it until you're looking at the Cross for the charity. Starting at the edge of the road, walk about seventeen paces. And I see it. A headstone that reads:

HENRY DARGER
1892–1973
Artist
Protector of Children

Someone has wedged a child's blue paintbrush into the edge of the headstone. I place it directly on the stone. I crouch there for some time.

I drive across River Road to her plot. I am compelled again to return to my mother's gravesite, even though I do not believe she is housed there.

I crouch at her headstone for a while. The gigantic statue of St. Francis nearby. My mother's favorite saint. A martyr. I pick at the grass and stare at the coral-colored headstone. On the left side, my mother's name. And then: Loving Wife and Mother.

I stare at the inscription for a long time.

My father has already had his name and birthdate engraved next to hers on their shared stone marker. Loving Husband and Father.

How he would like to be remembered. How he would like her to be remembered. How I imagine she would have liked to have been remembered as well.

I roll a blade of grass around in my palm.

Carving into this amorphous mass of marble, can a figure emerge.

I think of Louise Bourgeois saying, *Every day you have to abandon the past or accept it. If you cannot accept it, you become a sculptor.*

I mutter, mutter, mutter.

(2003–2016)

NOTES AND SOURCES:

The following is an attempt to cite the voices that flitted through my head as I set about this work of mutter and memories, voices that are not my own or ancestral. These fragments are, at times, lines committed to memory and potentially altered in the process. Other times these texts and pieces of reworded information are a result of fervent yet lapsed and inexact research, on the Internet, in libraries, and archives official and otherwise. My hope is that this list of sources whose origins are not clear in the main text will not unnecessarily complicate the sifting through the rubble that is reading.

A NOTE ON SOME MAIN FIGURES AND CONCEPTS:

Henry Darger

I had the opportunity to research at the study center of the Intuit Gallery, that contains microfilms of Darger's archive and his recon-structed room. There I read many of his weather reports and journals for an essay that originally appeared in the now-defunct journal *Paper & Carriage*. An important source of biographical information, and passages from *The History of My Life* and his writings from *The Realms of the Unreal* are taken from Michael Bonesteel's *Henry Darger: Art and Selected Writings*. I also read John MacGregor's book on Darger for background, as well as quoted from it. I also visited many of his haunts in Lincoln Park, guided by online fans of Darger. In thinking about Darger, I was also indebted to my friend-ship with the poet Rebecca Loudon and the artist Angela Simione (whose charcoal drawing of Elsie Paroubek hangs in my office).

Louise Bourgeois

The writings and artwork of Louise Bourgeois, and her thinking and making art through and out of trauma, were integral to the work. I took pilgrimages to her retrospective when it was in London at the Tate and New York at the Guggenheim while writing *Mutter*, and it was these in-person encounters with her *Cells* that helped catalyze the form and rhythm of the work. I also quote liberally from her interviews and writing, collected in *Destruction of the Father Reconstruction of the Father: Writings and Interviews 1923–1997* and the Tate Louise Bourgeois catalogue.

Joan of Arc

My information about Joan of Arc was discovered through reading several biographies, as well as inspired by Carl Theodor Dreyer's 1928 silent film *The Passion of Joan of Arc*, starring Renée Falconetti. I gleaned information about the shooting of the film through Internet sources. There were many works that deeply inspired and catalyzed *Mutter*—but especially Theresa Hak Kyung Cha's *Dictee*, and my use of Falconetti's image from the Dreyer film is a quote from and homage to this work of mother-myths.

Mary Todd Lincoln

Some of my information on Mary Todd Lincoln was gathered from attending the exhibit of the Lincoln Museum in Springfield, although at times the curatorial notes are reworded. I also found information about Lincoln's insanity trial from numerous sources online.

Civil War–era Photography

I spent a day researching at Duke University's Rubenstein Library. Much of the material dealing with postmortem photography I gleaned from the trilogy *Sleeping Beauty: Memorial Photoraphy in America*, edited by Stanley Burns.

Barbara Loden/Marilyn Monroe

Still seeded into the text is a reflection of the actress/director Barbara Loden and her twinning with Marilyn Monroe, Arthur Miller's play "After the Fall," based on Marilyn and starring Loden, Elia Kazan's 1961 film *Splendor in the Grass*, his memoir *The Arrangement*, about Loden, Marilyn Monroe's *NYT* obit, and Barbara Loden's own 1970 film *Wanda*, but mostly subtextual and a lot of the other stuff (Arthur Miller's institutionalized child, Marilyn Monroe's FBI files and auction of her clothes, both reported in *Vanity Fair* articles) are absent from this version of the text.

OTHER MAIN THREADS/FIGURES NOW ABANDONED, ABSENT FROM THIS VERISON OF THE TEXT:

The Torture Archive and testimony of the Tipton Three and The Qahtani Logs; a meditation on the Abu Ghraib photographs, gleaned from wathcing Errol Morris's documentary *Standard Operating Procedure*; the language of the memos of the Bush adminstration regarding torture and Jenny Holzer's series dealing with redacted documentation; a history of the Illinois asylums at Elgin and Manteno; Philippe Pinel's ideas of *traitement moral* as discussed in Michel Foucault's *The History of Madness*; a weaving in of Marguerite Duras's screenplay for *Hiroshima, mon Amour*;

the auctioning of Mary Todd Lincoln's clothes, her dabblings in spiritualism, the memoir of her seamstress and confidante Elizabeth Keckley, a former slave; both Sontag and Bataille's meditation on the photograph of Fou-Tchou-Li, as he suffered from *lingchi*, or death by a thousand cuts; various Nazi records.

OTHER UNCITED SOURCES (IN ORDER, MORE OR LESS)

The stations of a woman's life. From Peter Handke's *A Sorrow Beyond Dreams.*

History is hysterical. From Roland Barthes's *Camera Lucida.*

No mother can ever have been more abstract than you are. From Violette Leduc's *La Bâtarde.*

With regard to many of these photographs, it was History which separated me from them.... From Roland Barthes's *Camera Lucida.*

It's true that a photograph is a witness, but a witness of something that is no more. From Roland Barthes's *Camera Lucida.*

My pain is the hidden side of my philosophy, its mute sister. From Julia Kristeva's *Black Sun.*

for you, no wound... Also from Roland Barthes's *Camera Lucida.*

An unknown person has written me... From Roland Barthes's *Camera Lucida.*

my stillborn manuscript, which I didn't know how or why to bury...
From Marie Chaix's *Summer of the Elder Tree*.

Let's go back again, open your belly and take me back. From Violette Leduc's *La Bâtarde*.

*What happened there was silence...*From Marguerite Duras's *The Lover*.

If I talk to you, I may break everything. But, that's not my fault; I can be very, very sorry afterwards. From Louise Bourgeois.

If we continue to speak the same language... From Luce Irigaray's *This Sex Which is Not One*.

Suddenly, a shock that penetrates even the roots of your hair... From Christa Wolf's *Patterns of Childhood*.

the beast, my mother, my love. From Marguerite Duras's *The Lover*.

Have you really not forgotten what it was like there?... From Nathalie Sarraute's *Enfances*

I think I'm beginning to see my life.... From Marguerite Duras's *The Lover*.

The UNDO *is the unraveling....* From Louise Bourgeois's text "I Do, I Undo, I Redo," collected in *Destruction of the Father Reconstruction of the Father: writings and Interviews 1923–1997*.

divining, through her own past... From Virginia Woolf's *To the Lighthouse*.

The scream does violence to the throat... From Catherine Clément's *Syncope: The Philosophy of Rapture.*

She is the woman who discharges the unspeakable things on behalf of the city. Quoted in Anne Carson's essay "The Gender of Sound" collected in *Glass, Irony and God.*

Each of us has their own rhythm of suffering. From Roland Barthes's *Mourning Diary.*

I have known the body of my mother, sick and then dying... From Roland Barthes's *Mourning Diary.*

Why did you leap from the tower at Beaurevoir? Reworded from the Orleans manuscript.

We were never intimate Mother and Children... From a letter by Emily Dickinson.

I never intended to deny my apparitions.... attributed to Joan of Arc.

She is thy mother; thou shalt not uncover her nakedness. From Leviticus.

I can't stop people from saying what they need to say. I don't know how to stop repetitions like these. From Claudia Rankine's *Don't Let Me Be Lonely: An American Lyric.*

It belongs to him, as much as his wedding. From Arthur Miller's play *After the Fall.*

ACKNOWLEDGMENTS

I would like to express gratitude to the many readers over the years of the various incarnations of this project, some who have offered specific interventions, and others for their encouragement along the way, all in different yet crucial forms, especially Sofia Samatar, Suzanne Scanlon, Suzanne Buffam, Danielle Dutton, Lidia Yuknavitch, Amina Cain, Bhanu Kapil, Angela Simione, Rebecca Loudon, Julie Carr, Lisa Pearson, Cal Morgan, Sofia Groopman, Suzanna Tamminen, Anne Marie Rooney, Ryan Ruby, Caroline Crumpacker, Siri Hustvedt, Moyra Davey, and Mel Flashman. To T. Clutch Fleischmann, for the example of their own marvelous book, *Syzygy, Beauty*, that also circles around Louise Bourgeois's *Cells*. For the gifted writers and thinkers in my Writing the Visual undergraduate seminar at Columbia University, who inspired me with the example of their own work and energized me to go back to this project and attempt it again. I am incredibly grateful to Hedi El Kholti and Chris Kraus for everything they do for literature at Semiotext(e), and for being the brilliant, insightful readers that they are, and for giving this misfit text a home.

To the wonderful librarians, library aides, and cultural workers everywhere I conducted research over the past decade, in thinking through this text, some of which does not appear in this book in its final form, namely in Chicago at the Spertus Institute, the Study Center at the Intuit Gallery, where the Henry Darger microfilms are housed, and the Newberry Library, and in Durham, North Carolina at Duke University. I would like to especially acknowledge the library aides and librarians at the Skokie, Illinois branch of Oakton Community College, who were always so cheerful and supportive about this adjunct humanities instructor taking out bags of heavy art and theory books through interlibrary loan a decade ago, during the time I was incubating this project and myself as a writer.

I am as always indebted to my partner and great love John Vincler, who has lived with this work as well since its inception more than a decade ago, who was the first person I sought out for advice when I wanted to begin writing the history of all of this, and did not know what form it would take, and who through the years has been always first reader, brilliant editor, and crucial confidante. Thank you for your tenderness and patience, with me, and with this work.

I was visited again by this work, after some absence, in the beginning of this year, and I gradually over the weeks of working intensely on it, this rush of lucidity, became aware of and rather stunned by the growing fact of my pregnancy. So this work feels not only dedicated to my mother, but to my future daughter, Leonora Gale, who as of typing this acknowledgment I have not yet met, but will soon. As I sit here and meditate on this marvel, this uncanniness, I feel the longing and melancholy of generations, especially to know that my mother will never meet her grandchild, whom she would have been so thrilled by. But there's a beauty to this heaviness as well, that I believe and hope has saturated this now final version of the book.

KZ, 6/24/2016